MULTICULTURAL
LITERATURE

A READER'S GUIDE TO
LORRAINE HANSBERRY'S

A Raisin in the Sun

PAMELA LOOS

Enslow Publishers, Inc.
40 Industrial Road
Box 398
Berkeley Heights, NJ 07922
USA
    http://www.enslow.com

Library of Congress Cataloging-in-Publication Data

Loos, Pamela. A reader's guide to Lorraine Hansberry's A raisin in the sun /
Pamela Loos.

    p. cm. — (Multicultural literature)

  Includes bibliographical references and index.

  ISBN-13: 978-0-7660-2830-2

  ISBN-10: 0-7660-2830-5

1. Hansberry, Lorraine, 1930-1965. Raisin in the sun—Juvenile literature.
2. African Americans in literature. I. Title.

  PS3515.A515R337 2007

  812'.54-dc22

                        2006017900

Printed in the United States of America

10 9 8 7 6 5 4 3 2 1

Supports the English/Language Arts and Literature curricula.

To Our Readers:

We have done our best to make sure all Internet addresses in this book were active
and appropriate when we went to press. However, the author and the publisher have
no control over and assume no liability for the material available on those Internet
sites or on other Web sites they may link to. Any comments or suggestions can be
sent by e-mail to comments@enslow.com or to the address on the back cover.

Illustration Credits: cover, pages 4 and 19: Everett Collection, Inc.; page 31:
Library of Congress; pages 50, 70, 82, 94, 106 and 113: Everett Collection, Inc.

Cover Illustration: Sidney Poitier and Claudia McNeil in a scene from the 1961
film *A Raisin in the Sun.* Courtesy of the Everett Collection, Inc.

Contents

Lorraine Hansberry

Art with Purpose

I was born in a depression after one world war, and came into my adolescence during another. While I was still in my teens the first atom bombs were dropped at Nagasaki and Hiroshima, and by the time I was twenty-three years old my government and that of the Soviet Union had entered into the worst conflict of nerves in human history—the Cold War. I have lost friends and relatives through cancer, lynching and war. I have been personally the victim of physical attack which was the offspring of racial and political hysteria.[1]

✻

As this description indicates, Lorraine Hansberry, the author of *A Raisin in the Sun,* was very much affected by both global and personal experiences.

Even at the young age of eight, the African-American girl experienced prejudice directly when her family moved into what had been a whites-only neighborhood. Here and in other areas at the time, homeowners controlled the types of fellow inhabitants living in their neighborhoods through the use of "racially restrictive covenants." These covenants were designed mostly to keep African Americans and Jewish people out of certain neighborhoods. White homeowners signed these covenants, which were agreements to not let particular people buy, rent, or lease homes from them. While the covenants were clearly discriminatory, in 1937 in Chicago they were still legal.

As more and more African Americans teemed into Chicago during the Depression, African-American neighborhoods became overburdened. Faced with this deteriorating situation, politically active African Americans such as Hansberry's parents decided to press for change. They thought that the time was ripe, because President Franklin D. Roosevelt had appointed more liberal judges to the Supreme Court. As the first step, Hansberry and others bought two homes in a white neighborhood, without letting the owners know they were selling to African Americans.

Once the two African-American families moved in to what had been an all-white neighborhood, the inhabitants took legal measures against the new families, saying they were prohibited from living in the neighborhood. In court, members of the National Association for the Advancement of Colored People (NAACP) argued for the African-American families, but the judge ruled against them, saying the families must move out of the neighborhoods. The NAACP appealed the case twice in higher courts. Despite losing both times the group took the case to the Supreme Court, believing its more liberal judges might sway the others in the families' favor. In fact, this court did rule in their favor. The court, however, did not go a step further—it did not make racially restrictive covenants illegal. Still, the justices' ruling did make it easier for minorities to fight such covenants and easier for such agreements to eventually be ruled illegal.

By the time all the court appeals had taken place, Lorraine's father, Carl Hansberry, had seen both his business and his health suffer because so much of his energy had been focused on the court battles. Additionally, the family had been terrorized by their neighbors. Lorraine herself had almost suffered what could have been a fatal head injury from a brick thrown by a prejudiced neighbor. In short, winning had come at a cost. But the Hansberrys were no average family. Indeed, from a young age, the children had been taught pride, not only in themselves but in their race. Throughout her life, Lorraine Hansberry would continue to fight in similar battles, standing up for her beliefs and/or bringing such beliefs to public attention through various forums. In fact, an African-American family considering moving into a white neighborhood would become the topic of her first play.

Born on May 19, 1930, in Chicago, Lorraine Hansberry was the fourth and youngest child born to Nannie Perry Hansberry and Carl Hansberry. Nannie was the daughter of a minister and had attended college, which few women of the time had. Carl was a successful real estate man. He and his wife bought properties in Chicago, converting them to affordable apartments consisting of a kitchen and a large room. By 1940, following the success of his court case against restrictive covenants, Carl ran for Congress but lost.

Both Carl and his wife were activists, and the family was frequently visited by well-known African Americans, including civil rights leader and scholar W.E.B. DuBois; actor and activist Paul Robeson;

musician Duke Ellington; Olympic gold medalist Jesse Owens; and poet Langston Hughes. The Hansberry children, even at a young age, were encouraged to engage in conversations on current topics, so they could learn how to present their arguments and could be shaped to become valuable citizens and leaders.

Lorraine first became interested in theater at Englewood High School in Chicago. After graduating in 1948, she attended the University of Wisconsin at Madison. It was there that she fell in love with the plays of Sean O'Casey and decided to pursue a life in theater. In February of 1950, though, Hansberry left the university. She studied at Roosevelt University in Chicago over the summer and in the fall moved to New York. There she worked on *Freedom*, the radical publication produced by Paul Robeson. It was in New York that she met Robert Nemiroff, a Jewish intellectual writer, during a protest at New York University against excluding blacks from university sports. They married on June 20, 1953. Hansberry studied at the New School for Social Research and also studied African culture and history with W.E.B. DuBois at the Jefferson School of Social Science. In 1956 Nemiroff sold a song, "Cindy, Oh Cindy," he had collaborated on and it became highly successful. Hansberry decided to work on her playwrighting on a full-time basis.[2]

Hansberry's first play, *A Raisin in the Sun*, provided a realistic portrayal of the hard lives of an African-American family living in Chicago's South Side who have a chance to move out of their segregated neighborhood. The play was produced on Broadway in 1959. It had presented some problems for the playwright, though. For example, while its cast and director were talented, they were a bit inexperienced. Also, since the play was considered a risky proposition because of its mostly African-American cast, it had taken nearly a year

to amass the money needed to produce it.
Prior to Broadway, the play had been performed
and done well, yet when its preview showed in
New York, the response was less than enthusiastic.
Despite this history, however, the Broadway
production proved quite a success.

The play garnered many distinctions for
Hansberry: At age twenty-nine, she was the first
African-American woman to have a play produced
on Broadway. Also, she was the youngest American
and the first African American to win the New
York Drama Critics Circle Award for the best play
of the year. The play ran on Broadway for almost
two years. It was published and produced in
more than thirty languages and brought many
African Americans to the theater. While some
of Hansberry's early screenplay versions of the
play were rejected, one was accepted. In 1961 the
film, starring most of the Broadway cast, won
a Cannes Film Festival Award and was nominated

for an award from the Screen Writers Guild for the screenplay. This success and attention provided Hansberry more venues for addressing the public. She spoke out for civil rights and the African fight against colonial rule.

Hansberry's second play, *The Sign in Sidney Brustein's Window*, opened in 1964. Critics gave it mixed reviews, and Hansberry's friends helped gather the funds to keep it running for 101 performances. Its last showing on January 12, 1965, was the night Hansberry died from cancer at the young age of thirty-four.

The author left work in progress, including some plays and *Toussaint*, an opera based on the life of the eighteenth-century Haitian leader by that name. In 1969 Nemiroff published and produced an off-Broadway montage of Hansberry's life, *To Be Young, Gifted, and Black*. It contained parts of her unpublished writings, speeches, and journal entries as well as sections from interviews. Despite their divorce in 1964, Nemiroff remained Hansberry's literary executor. He adapted her play *Les Blancs*, a work about African liberation, and had it produced on Broadway in 1970. In 1972 he edited and published *Les Blancs: The Collected Last Plays of Lorraine Hansberry*, which contained *The Drinking Gourd*, *Les Blancs*, and *What Use Are Flowers?* In 1973, he produced and wrote *Raisin*, a musical version of *A Raisin in the Sun*, with Charlotte Zaltzberg. It won a Tony Award for best musical. In 1989, the American Playhouse produced *A Raisin in the Sun* for television.

LITERARY EXECUTOR
A person appointed to manage the literary property of an author who has died.

The famed author James Baldwin wrote of Hansberry: "Lorraine made no bones about asserting that art has a purpose, and that its purpose was action: that it contained the 'energy which could change things.'"[3]

CHAPTER 2

Plot and Other Elements

In *A Raisin in the Sun,* we see a poor, African-American family struggling to live in Chicago's South Side, sometime after World War II but before 1959. Five family members are squeezed into a small apartment and have to share a bathroom with others in the building. The family is excited about a $10,000 life insurance check that is soon to arrive. While Ruth and Beneatha say the check is Mama's to use as she wishes, Walter has his sights set on using part of the money to invest in a liquor store, so he can leave behind his subservient job as a chauffeur and live the

American dream. Mama and Beneatha are against his plan, and through most of the play Walter is keenly distressed because he believes no one understands him. He accuses most people, including his family, of not being big thinkers like he is. Rather early in the play, though, we see that both Mama and Beneatha are intent on fulfilling their own dreams. Mama plans to buy a small house, and Beneatha is going to school to become a doctor.

AMERICAN DREAM
The notion that anyone in the United States, even if he or she starts out with almost nothing, can become prosperous.

Tension builds as the family waits for the check and to find out what, exactly, Mama will do with it. For the family, $10,000 is a lot of money. We see family members, tired of living in their seemingly hopeless situation, arguing with each other about what is to be done with the money. Adding to the tension is the fact that Ruth is pregnant. Because she feels the family's finances are strained, she has gone to see a doctor about getting an abortion, although she is extremely upset about the idea of losing her own baby.

Ruth has no confidence in her husband's friends that he wants to go into business with. Still, because she feels her marriage deteriorating, she asks Mama if she can give Walter some money for the business. Ruth knows it will make him happy and take the strain off their marriage. Mama remains opposed to giving Walter any money, however, and instead puts down a payment on a house. She also wants to use some of the money for Beneatha's education. This tears Walter to shreds, and when Mama realizes just how much he is affected, she gives in and tells Walter that while she has made the deposit on the house, he is to take the rest of the money and put part of it aside for Beneatha and use the rest however he decides. Walter is pulled out of despair now that he is trusted and able to move toward his dream.

All of the rest of the family members are excited about moving into the new house.

The family happily packs but is visited by a guest while Mama is out. The visitor, Karl Lindner, says he is from the welcoming committee in the neighborhood where Mama has bought the new house. While the family members have been concerned about Mama buying the house in a neighborhood where African Americans are not wanted, they do not immediately realize that the visitor has bad intentions. He tells those gathered that all would be better off if they did not move into the neighborhood, and he offers to buy the house back from them at a higher price. The family members are outraged, and Walter proudly chases the man away. Soon after, Walter's friend Bobo visits and the family learns that Walter and Bobo have given money to another friend to pay people off so they can get their liquor license. The supposed friend has taken off with the money. Walter had

The Younger family arrives at their new home in the 1961
film adaptation of Lorraine Hansberry's *A Raisin in the Sun.*

given him not only the money Mama had said
he could use but also the money that Mama
wanted earmarked for Beneatha's education.
The family is shocked and devastated.

At various points in the play, Beneatha brings
in men from school and one, Joseph Asagai, an

African native, tries to convince Beneatha that losing the money is not as bad as she thinks. His presence throughout the play gets Beneatha interested in Africa. He makes the audience realize that it is not only African Americans who are suffering but that native Africans are suffering as well.

Walter tells the family his plan that will make them no longer part of the "taken" category, the category of those who are always being taken advantage of. He calls Lindner back and tells the family he plans to play the part of the deferential, accommodating African-American man and accept Lindner's offer. Before the family can talk Walter out of his plan, however, Lindner arrives. When Mama tells Travis he must stay to hear what his father plans to say, Walter, who was already hesitant about his plan, changes his mind. He explains to Lindner that he comes from a proud family, that they all work hard, and that he cannot accept Lindner's offer. The family is greatly relieved, proud that Walter has done the right thing, and, as Mama says, finally become a man.

While the family is happy and excited at the play's end, some have argued that this ending is unsatisfying, since the family members are only moving into another situation where they will be unhappy victims of prejudice. Certainly the family has been in a state of despair while stuck in their small apartment—in a very small space with roaches, little sun, the burden of having to share a bathroom, and renting rather than owning their own place. While they have been truly struggling in the apartment, one could argue that at least they have not been physically attacked or felt unsafe, as they undoubtedly will be in their new home, considering Lindner's comments.

How can the family be happy then? Are they naïve, not truly realizing what they are getting into? "Most Chicagoans ... had no idea of the situation's volatility. For much of the 1940s the major newspapers, at the request of the Chicago

Commission on Human Relations, would simply not report the occurrence of these riots,"[1] the Chicago Public Library website reports. Yet certainly Hansberry herself knew what it was like to move into a neighborhood where African Americans were unwanted.

The family in Hansberry's play, too, is not naïve. When Mama tells Ruth and Walter where she has bought the house, they are shocked and make comments that show they know living in the neighborhood will be a trying experience. In short, then, they know what they are in for. At the same time, the family is strong. They are proud of their family and their heritage and are determined and powerful. As a result, they believe no one can push them around. They will own their own land and home. At the same time, they are chipping away at prejudice. If they and others are willing to do the chipping, life will become fairer and easier for future generations.

When Mama bought the house, though, she was not looking to make a stand. She said she only bought the house where she did because the same house in an African-American neighborhood cost more. In Hansberry's view, it seems, it is impossible to suppress the basic human instinct of wanting what is fair and what is best for one's loved ones. Hansberry also knows that prejudice and its ramifications cannot be resolved easily or quickly. Indeed, the family's move is a reinforcement of that. Change will come, only very slowly, and it might not even seem like progress at first. As Asagai says, sometimes there are even steps backward:

> I will go home and much of what I will have to say will seem strange to the people of my village ... But I will teach and work and things will happen, slowly and swiftly. At times it will seem that nothing changes at all ... and then again ... the sudden dramatic events which make history leap into the future. And then quiet again. Retrogression even. Guns, murder, revolution. And I even will have moments when

I wonder if the quiet was not better than all that death and hatred. But I will look about my village at the illiteracy and disease and ignorance and I will not wonder long.[2]

If the family had moved out of its poor, unhappy life to a much improved situation, this would have seemed unrealistic. For African Americans during the time of Hansberry's play, there were few, if any, easy answers. Hansberry makes this sense of foreboding clear—by the reactions from the family members when they hear where Mama has bought the house and by Lindner's antagonizing visit. At the same time, this foreboding also appears in more subtle ways. For example, in the opening of the play, when Walter reads the paper, he reads that there has been a bombing. The fact that such a disturbing occurrence is announced so early in the play puts the audience on edge.

Indeed, Hansberry's play was praised for its realism. The family's situation was seen as a true portrayal of African-Americans' lives at the end of the 1950s. Aside from the situation shown, the realistic portrayal is apparent in the characters and their dialogue. The family speaks the way a family at the time and in its position would. Beneatha and her beaus speak differently than the rest of the family, as would those who are college educated. The family also talks about whites and the African-American situation, as any such family would, but as almost no family in a play did at the time this play was produced or before.

For example, when Ruth seems to be sick, Mama says she will call her employer and say that Ruth has the flu, since this is something the employer will understand and because "otherwise they think you been cut up or something when you tell 'em you sick."[3] In other comments, Ruth, when she learns where the new house is located, says "'course I ain't one never been 'fraid of no crackers."[4] We do not only get a perspective on African

Americans' views of whites, though, we also see African-Americans' views of themselves. Walter, for example, makes comments about the two groups, disparaging both. Beneatha, too, makes negative comments about rich African Americans, saying the only thing worse than rich whites are rich African Americans. The comments show there is no one perspective or one true view of the races, again reinforcing the realism of the play and also pointing out how foolish stereotypes are. African Americans felt the play had given them a voice. As James Baldwin wrote about the play:

> [N]o one can gainsay its importance. What is relevant here is that I had never in my life seen so many black people in the theater. And the reason was that never before, in the entire history of the American theater, had so much of the truth of black people's lives been seen on the stage. Black people ignored the theater because the theater had always ignored them.[5]

CHAPTER 3

Themes

Hansberry's *A Raisin in the Sun* has numerous themes, or topics of discussion, to provoke her audience. Certainly two central ones are concerned with dreams and pride. Almost every character in the play has some dream, despite the seeming hopelessness of the family's situation, and these various dreams are brought up frequently. The intense pride the family members have in themselves and their race overall is what helps make it possible for them to hold onto their dreams and not completely despair. As one critic explained:

> *Set against a backdrop of overt racism and pervasive*
> *housing discrimination in the 1950s, Hansberry's play manages*

to recover and sustain ethical idealism amid conditions, per-
sonal and societal, that would make fatalistic surrender
understandable. . . . It is a play about distress, futility, and
tragedy, but also about hope and pride and what kind of
conviction and commitment it takes to bring hope out of hope-
lessness, courage out of fear, and idealism out of fatalism.[1]

Part of the appeal of the play, also, is its ability to show the true horrors of prejudice—its suffocating effects and its near destruction of individuals, who suffer severely because of prejudice's restrictions and resultant poverty. As one writer notes about the stifling conditions, "Walter blames himself, his wife and his mother for what he sees as his personal failure. And only at the end of the play does it become possible for him to realize that there is a puppeteer manipulating him, a puppeteer who brought him

FATALISTIC
Feeling powerless because of the belief that life is predetermined.

dangerously close to destroying his family and him-self."² At the play's climactic ending, even though the family will be moving into a neighborhood where it will face new problems, jubilation within the family and audience occurs because Walter has not given in to prejudice. He has confirmed his belief, pride, and dignity in his own self, family, and race. Hansberry is saying that we all must put up similar fights, whether in Chicago or Africa, whether in the fifties or today, and that part of what makes that possible is not only our belief in our-selves but the support we get from our family and others who love us.

It is this battle between remaining hopeful or giving in to despair that Hansberry keeps remind-ing her audience of as she repeatedly brings up the theme of dreams and relates the various dreams of family members. Indeed, before the play even begins, we can read the Langston Hughes poem printed at the beginning of the published play, from which Hansberry derived her title. Part of it follows:

> *What happens to a dream deferred?*
> *Does it dry up*
> *Like a raisin in the sun?*[3]

The poem sets a disturbing tone for the dream theme. There is no good answer to the question of what happens to a dream that is put off, according to the poem. Several horrid possibilities are suggested, with the final one being the most violent and destructive. As the play begins, then, we wonder how Hansberry's vision will unfold. Will someone, or more than one person, be pushed to explode? Yet when the play opens, we quickly feel that all cannot be as completely hopeless as the ominous poem warned, for there is a check coming to the family and it obviously is for a large amount. The check, which various characters excitedly bring up, signals that dreams are in

LANGSTON HUGHES

Langston Hughes (1902–1967), one of the first African Americans to gain attention for his writing, wrote the poem that inspired Hansberry's title her play *A Raisin in the Sun*. He was a famous African-American poet, known for providing vivid images of the African-American experience. His work influenced many who came after him, including poet Gwendolyn Brooks and others. He published ten volumes of poetry, as well as fiction, plays, essays, screenplays, and autobiographical works; he also translated poetry. Before *A Raisin in the Sun*, his play *Mulatto* had the longest run on Broadway of any African-American playwright.

Hughes was born in Missouri and until the age of twelve was brought up mostly by his grandmother. His parents divorced, and he settled with his mother and grandmother in Cleveland. He had quite a varied life, living in a number of locations and holding an array of jobs. For example, he worked on a freighter traveling to Africa; as a busboy in a hotel in Washington, D.C.; as a cook in Paris; and as a newspaper correspondent in the Spanish Civil War, until he began to write full time. Hughes gained many awards and honors for his writing and worked to help other African-American writers as well. He also became known for a comic character he created, Jesse B. Semple, usually called Simple, who appeared in Hughes' columns in different newspapers as well as in short stories and on the stage. Simple was known for his simple wisdom and for outwitting the supposedly more educated members of society.

fact possible, despite the family's current situation.

While Hansberry clearly feels people must never lose hope and must have dreams, she also shows that dreams must not be too far a stretch from reality. Walter and Beneatha never seem to think about this, but Mama does. When she learns that Walter has lost the money, she decides the family should not move into the new house, and wonders why she always has reached for too much: "Lord, ever since I was a little girl, I always remembers people saying, 'Lena—Lena Eggleston, you aims too high all the time. You needs to slow down and see life a little more like it is. Just slow down some.' That is what they always used to say down home—'Lord, that Lena Eggleston is a high-minded thing. She'll get her due one day!'"[4]

Similarly, Hansberry points out that people cannot be dreamers only but need to be smart, wise, and realistic as well. The fact that Walter has no experience in owning a liquor store is something

Mama points out and surely is something that the audience thinks about. How can he be so confident about owning the store when he seems to have no experience in this area, we wonder. Similarly, when he describes his dreams of being a top executive or when he speaks of being envious of the white men hatching big deals in fancy restaurants, he does not stop to think that he lacks the knowledge that may be needed to do these things. His wife, Ruth, serves as the one who is more realistic, yet Walter sees her only as an impediment. Hansberry shows her value though, since Ruth is the one who realizes all along that Willy cannot be trusted and this turns out to be the case. Even on a very small scale, we see Ruth as being the realist and Walter as the ultimate dreamer. This is shown when Walter proudly gives his son not only the money he needs for school but extra money. Walter does this because he does not want his son to have worries about practical things like money. He wants him to be able to treat himself, to think big. Only later does Walter realize that giving his son the money leaves him with no money in his own pocket. Walter then has to go to Ruth, the practical, careful one, to ask for money.

Another theme that repeatedly occurs in the play is that of understanding. For instance, Walter many times cries out that his wife, mother, and fellow African Americans do not understand him. Beneatha also says no one in the family understands her but that she does not expect them to. Indeed, at various points, Walter, Mama, and Ruth all admit they do not understand Beneatha; for instance, they do not see why she would not want to marry the rich George Murchison. Aside from Walter's great agitation over not being understood, Mama is quite upset that she cannot understand her children and the way the world is changing.

In many ways, part of the lack of understanding has to do with generational issues. Mama makes an effort to try to understand, listening to Beneatha about George Murchison and also listening to her son try to explain his own internal turmoil. Her listening pays off, because she does see Beneatha's perspective on George and does realize she needs to help Walter by trusting him and letting him have power in the home. At the same time, while Walter and Beneatha are both products of a newer generation than Mama's, they still rely on some of the values that she instilled in them—pride in one's self and one's race and standing up for what is right, for example. Hansberry seems to be saying, again, that a balance is necessary. As the world moves forward in time, it still cannot neglect its past. Additionally, we cannot assume that anything that is new is better.

In the play, we clearly see the prejudice not just against African Americans but against women. Walter has his own negative and narrow views of women, and so does George. At the same time, we see three very strong women in the play, coming at life from their own directions. Beneatha, the most liberal and the one who embraces the newest ideas, plans to be a doctor and may not even get married. Yet later, when Joseph visits, he pokes fun at feminists and points out that they still have a long way to go. His comment is not one made to belittle but an observation and one designed to get Beneatha to think. His view (and George's) serve to show that even in the new generation there still can be widely varying perspectives. George wants kisses from Beneatha, not too much talk. He is blatantly impolite, telling her she cannot wear her African garb on their date, for example. Joseph, on the other hand, brings Beneatha the presents she wanted—the very African garb George looks down on. Joseph also loves her talk and is enchanted with her personality.

Aside from their differing perspectives on

Beneatha, George and Joseph contrast with each other in many other ways. Most notably, George laughs at Beneatha's interest in Africa, while Joseph is intent on going back to Africa, his home, to help those there. Joseph is willing to give up his life for a cause; George is not concerned about causes. He is from a rich family and we assume he has had an easy life. While Joseph is a thinker, George sees college not as an opportunity to learn about and enjoy thinking but as just a necessary step along the way. George, then, serves as an example of an African-American man who has not had to struggle, seemingly has not had to push dreams aside, and is small-minded, rude, and uninteresting. Perhaps Hansberry is saying that while certainly people should not live a life of daily struggle, an easy life is not always the ideal either.

A scene from the 1961 film adaptation of *A Raisin in the Sun*, featuring Ruby Dee as Ruth and John Fiedler as Mark Lindner.

CHAPTER 4

Dramatic Devices

While Hansberry's play has been described as realistic for its portrayal of complex rather than stereotyped African Americans and for its look into how African Americans lived as a result of prejudice, the playwright does not end up with a play that simply mimics what could have been recorded by anyone with a video camera at the time. More specifically, while Hansberry's characters and their situations are realistic, dramatic techniques also are used so the play can work on a stage and so the playwright's ideas can be effectively communicated.

For instance, the staging of the play and the set design reinforce the idea that the family feels trapped and has felt this way for some time. In terms of staging, the play takes place entirely in the family's apartment. While events that affect the family occur outside the apartment, the audience never sees outside the apartment. For example, Walter goes out to drink and talk to his buddies, Mama goes out to find a house, and Beneatha goes on dates, yet none of this is shown. Instead the characters return to the apartment and tell what they did. By keeping the action in the apartment only, Hansberry reinforces the confined feeling, namely that the family is stuck in this apartment, that their life is not changing or getting better. Additionally, with all the action taking place in the apartment, Hansberry emphasizes that one's family members are always there—whether one is sick of them or one needs their support.

The very look of the apartment also reinforces

the family's being tired and worn out from their situation. Specifically, Hansberry says the furniture is strategically placed to hide worn spots on the rug and that the furniture is covered in doilies and other covers, to suggest that its original upholstery is worn and faded. "Weariness has, in fact, won in this room," Hansberry writes in the stage directions. "Everything has been polished, washed, and sat on, used, scrubbed too often."[1]

The family's feeling of confinement and also its lack of money is reinforced by the fact that the family is squeezed in a small space. Ruth and Walter's room "in the beginning of the life of this apartment was probably a breakfast room."[2] Travis sleeps on the couch, and Mama and Beneatha must share a room. In the main living area—the living room and kitchen area—there is only one small window, again reinforcing a feeling of confinement.

The effects of a lack of money are also pointed out by the fact that the family has to share a bathroom, which is shown to be quite a frustrating burden. Every day they are literally in a race for something that should have readily been at their disposal. As Julius Lester explained, "It [*A Raisin in the Sun*] goes right to the core of practically every black family in the ghettos of Chicago, New York, Los Angeles and elsewhere. Whether they have a picture of Jesus, Martin Luther King, or Malcolm X on the lead-painted walls of their rat-infested tenement, all of them want to get the hell out of there as quickly as they can."[3]

Hansberry also is conscious of how she reveals information to her audience. For instance, she creates suspense and holds the audience's interest by giving small pieces of information, keeping the audience guessing. Specifically, when the play opens, Walter asks Ruth about a check with great interest and a short while later Travis does as well, but the audience has no knowledge of why they are so interested in this or how much the check is for. We then find out that the check is Mama's and that Walter wants to invest it in a liquor store. Only when Mama, the last of the main characters to appear on stage, enters do we learn that the check is for the sizable amount of $10,000 and that it is an insurance check Mama is receiving for the death of her husband. Then Hansberry reveals that Mama does have some idea of what she wants to use it for—to purchase a house and for Beneatha's education. Since we know how intense Walter is about his dreams, we know a big confrontation is on the way.

Similarly, Hansberry builds suspense about Ruth. In the opening of the play, her husband asks her what is wrong; shortly after, Mama asks her the same thing and says since Ruth looks so poorly that she should stay home from work. At the end of the scene, Ruth nearly faints, so we know that something serious is going on. The scene closes with Mama rushing toward Ruth to help her. Even when the next scene opens, though, the audience does not immediately find out what is wrong with Ruth. Before Ruth comes in, Mama guesses that the woman is pregnant, inspiring the audience to speculate as well. Ruth arrives and does confirm that she is pregnant, but only later do we learn that she has not been to the doctor to check on the baby's health. Mama senses trouble and asks Ruth where she has been, but Walter enters and the conversation is interrupted, again extending the suspense.

CRESCENDO
The peak of an increase in intensity or volume.

In another instance, Hansberry builds suspense when Walter's friend Bobo arrives at the apartment. Bobo has some news and drags out the telling of it because it is bad news and he knows Walter will be extremely upset. As Walter tries to get the news from Bobo, Walter becomes more and more agitated, realizing something must really be wrong. This agitation, from the most volatile character in the play, builds to a crescendo, and we also watch how other characters react to Bobo's story, which ends with the revelation that his and Walter's supposed friend Willy has stolen their money. The impact is even more intense in Walter's case, since his family had been against the liquor store venture and since he also lost the money he was told to save for Beneatha.

Aside from using staging, design, and suspense to create the proper mood and rhythm and emphasize key points, Hansberry uses symbolism as well. A quite subtle example of Hansberry's use of symbolism occurs when she has two conversations going on between two groups of characters, each conversation at first seeming to be unrelated to the other. In this instance, Mama and Beneatha are talking about trying to get rid of roaches and how impossible it is. At the same time, Walter is on the phone with Willy talking about their business plan. Especially by the end of the play, when we learn that Willy has stolen Walter's and Bobo's money, we realize that the roach—a creature that most people find detestable and work to get rid of—is actually symbolic of Willy.

More obvious in the play is the symbol of Mama's plant. Whereas the conversation about the roaches may not be readily recognized as symbolic, because the plant is mentioned numerous times and has the spotlight at the end of the play, an audience should realize it is a symbol. The plant is not so healthy, but Mama carefully tends to it, checking on it at various points, commenting on how it really should have more sun, and tenderly wrapping it so that it will not get damaged in transit to the new home. The plant is symbolic of the family's own life. The family struggles and literally needs more sun and other essentials to help it live. At the same time, Mama loves, cherishes, and tends to the needs of the family members as best she can. (Notice that her plan to buy the house will benefit them all.) While Beneatha is surprised to see that Mama plans on taking her raggedy plant to the new home, by the end of the play, when Beneatha makes this comment, we realize that taking the plant is exactly what we would expect Mama to do. She has always nurtured her family and will do the same on the plant.

As mentioned, Mama comments on the sun in relation to her scraggy plant, but Ruth also mentions the sun, asking Mama if the new house will have lots of it. Just as plants need sun to grow, humans need sunlight for bodily processes. Additionally, sun implies happiness whereas lack of sun implies a dreariness and despair. Also, the sun rises at the beginning of each day and so has come to symbolize new beginnings.

Just as plants and humans need sun, they also need food. Both Ruth and Mama speak of food and offer it to help others. Mama, for example,

SYMBOLISM

Rather than just making a statement themselves or having their characters make a direct statement, writers sometimes use symbols to get their ideas across. While at times the technique can be frustrating to some readers or audiences, with experience they learn how to notice symbolism and usually find that it makes a work much more rewarding. Writers have numerous ways to get their messages to audiences and audiences usually pick up on the more direct messages (at a key climactic moment in a play, for example) and from there can see where the writer is leading them and recognize the more subtle symbolic messages. Over time, readers also come to learn some traditional symbols and can branch out from there. For example, a storm in a play often is a sign of something disturbing happening or about to happen. While at different points in history and in different cultures items have taken on different significance, and while symbols may be able to be interpreted in more than one way, a good reader realizes symbols fit in with the overall themes of the work.

says Ruth should eat better and take care of herself when she sees Ruth looking poorly. She also tells Joseph Asagai to visit so she can feed him. When she mentions this to him, though, it seems it is not so much out of concern over his health as the fact that his family is far away and he needs a mother-type figure to supply some nourishment.

Although the family members are poor, they are not so poor that they go hungry, and food is one thing that the mothering females in the play can always offer. In the play's opening, even though Walter is not interested in eggs, Ruth keeps telling him to eat them. Similarly, later when she offers him milk he is again not interested. She explains her feeling of desperation, saying that food is the one thing she can offer to help him. Again food comes up as symbolic when Joseph explains that he calls Beneatha a name that roughly translates to mean "the one for whom food is not enough." In his mind, Beneatha needs much more than literal nourishment from food; she hungers for knowledge and growth and new ideas.

A scene from the 1961 film adaptation of *A Raisin in the Sun*, featuring Claudia McNeil as Lena Younger.

CHAPTER 5

Lena

Lorraine Hansberry provided a description of Lena Younger as a determined fighter:

> *Lena Younger, the mother, is the black matriarch incarnate, the bulwark of the Negro family since slavery, the embodiment of the Negro will to transcendence. It is she, who in the mind of the black poet scrubs the floors of a nation in order to create black diplomats and university professors. It is she, while seeming to cling to traditional restraints, who drives the young on into the fire hoses.*[1]

Lena (called "Mama" by her children in the play) is strong and proud like the others. She

wants to help her children live good lives, hope-
fully ones that are easier than hers has been.
Her husband has only recently died and she takes
his place as the powerful leader of the family,
one who instructs them on right and wrong,
what they should say, do, and believe.

Lena has had a hard life but does not
complain about it. She reveals
how she watched her husband
work himself literally
to death, how she saw him
so often filled with despair.
She tells how she and her husband had
planned to live in the small apartment only for
a short time but were never able to afford to move
into something better. In her day, she explains,
African Americans had different concerns than
her children currently seem to have. They had
to worry about the very real possibility of being
lynched, for example. While Lena mostly is

MATRIARCH
A female leader of a
family or other group.

concerned with her own adult children, she also at times pushes Ruth to make sure she is treating Travis, Lena's grandson, the way he should be treated. Lena does not back down when Ruth is disturbed by her questioning. But perhaps Lena's ultimate display of toughness occurs when she buys a home for the family in a neighborhood that has been off limits to African Americans. She knows the family will probably suffer as a result but also knows her family deserves to live in the best home for the money they have available.

Lena clearly takes charge in the household. She will not allow her adult daughter to speak against God. She on her own decides what to do with the insurance money. She tells her son what to say to his wife when she is considering an abortion. At the same time, however, Lena is a great nurturer. She sees that something is wrong with

TRANSCENDENCE
The quality or state of being beyond the limits of ordinary experience.

Ruth and tells her she will do the ironing so Ruth does not have to. Lena also worries about fights in the house, tells her daughter to put on a robe to keep warm, has a soft spot for her grandson, and tells Joseph he must come by for a good home-cooked meal since he is so far away from his own home. Aside from caring for the family, she is intent on caring for her plant and never gives up on it, despite the fact that it is so scraggy and gets little sun. While she is horrified about Walter losing so much of the family's money and physically attacks him without thinking, she regains control and thinks about the situation. She returns to her loving self and gives one of the most moving speeches in the play, directing it at Beneatha, who appears unable to forgive her brother:

> *There is always something left to love. And if you ain't learned that, you ain't learned nothing.* (Looking at her) *Have you cried for that boy today? ... Child, when do you think is the time to love somebody the most; when they*

done good and made things easy for everybody? Well then, you ain't through learning—because that ain't the time at all. It's when he's at his lowest and cannot believe in hisself 'cause the world done whipped him so. When you starts measuring somebody, measure him right, child, measure him right. Make sure you done taken into account what hills and valleys he come through before he got to wherever he is.[2]

This speech, while showing how Lena values love and a supportive family, also shows she is wise. She has lived long enough to know that we all make mistakes and need forgiveness and understanding. Similarly, Lena shows she is wise about people and the world when she guesses Ruth is pregnant and notices how Ruth slips when she talks about the doctor, indicating she has not been to her regular doctor but to talk with some-one about having an abortion. Lena is also wise enough to realize that when things are going wrong, even when you are not sure why, you have to do something. She tells Ruth she put money toward the house because she had to do something to get people in the house to stop thinking about killing babies and wishing each other dead.

And ultimately, while Lena keeps saying she does not understand what is going on with her children and they also feel she does not understand them, she is smart enough to understand how to help prod her son to do what is right at the end of the play. To do this, she reminds him that even when members of the family were slaves or sharecroppers they could not be given money to keep them from doing what they were rightfully allowed to do. Aside from reminding Walter of his ancestry, she reminds him of his own son. When Mr. Lindner is at the door and the family feels Walter will cave in to the man's pressure to keep the family out of his neighborhood, Lena purposefully tells Travis to stay and listen to what his father is going to say to the visitor. She guesses, correctly, that Walter will stand up for himself and his family while his son is there.

While Lena is concerned that she does not understand her children, this example shows that she does know that her children are still proud people. Hansberry portrays Lena as someone of a different generation who still does want to connect with newer generations. In some ways she appears behind the times, such as when she talks to Ruth about Walter's dream of owning the liquor store. She says as part of her reasoning against it that her family have never been business folk. Similarly, when Beneatha talks to her about Africa, Lena asks why she should know anything about that. Also, while other family members may believe in God, Lena is the one that calls on him for strength and insists that no one deny his existence while in her house.

While we see these differences between Lena and the others, we also see that Lena is openminded, listens to her children, and does come to understand them in some respects. For example, she does not initially believe knowledge about Africa is important. But when Joseph arrives, she speaks to him about Africa, telling him nearly the very same things Beneatha has told her just moments before. This indicates how much Lena really was listening to her daughter and how she wants to learn.

Additionally, Lena shows that she is seeing her daughter differently when she accepts her daughter's view that George Murchison is not the person she should marry. Beneatha gives her perspective, and Lena, rather than questioning her daughter, trusts her judgment. In a smaller way, too, when her daughter questions why Lena takes so much care with a scrawny plant, Lena explains that it is a way to express herself, using the words Beneatha used to describe her own interests earlier in the play. While earlier in the play Lena had laughed when Beneatha had talked about expressing herself, now we see that Lena has come around. She sees that people need to have outlets, not just be caught up in the tortuous grind of living.

The significant change in Lena comes about in her view of her son. After she puts the money down on the house, she says she did it believing it would make life better for the whole family. But when she sees how disturbed Walter is about her decision, she feels guilty and believes she must do something more. She realizes that he feels completely oppressed and says that she has been adding to that, which she says is a mistake. She reverses her earlier decision of just using the money for the house and Beneatha's education. Instead, she tells her son to take the money, put some aside for Beneatha but use the rest however he decides. She realizes he needs to have some power of his own:

Mama *I'm telling you to be the head of this family from now on like you supposed to be.*

Walter (Stares at the money) *You trust me like that, Mama?*

Mama *I ain't never stop trusting you. Like I ain't never stop loving you.*[3]

Despite the fact that Lena has been against her son becoming a businessman and against his selling liquor, she sees that she must help him and that the best way to do that is to give him the money and turn authority over to him. Although Walter gets taken and loses the money, Lena at the end of the play is very proud of him for having stood up to Mr. Lindner. Her understanding has allowed Walter to grow.

CHAPTER 6

Walter

"Here I am a giant—surrounded by ants! Ants who cannot even understand what it is the giant is talking about."[1] Walter Younger, Mama's oldest child, yells this at George Murchison, a visitor. Yet it hardly matters who Walter says this to or when in the play he says it, for he makes similar statements at numerous points. In short, the statement sums up his vision and his great frustration. Hansberry describes him in the play: "He is a lean, intense young man in his middle thirties, inclined to quick nervous movements and erratic speech habits—and always in his voice there is a quality of indictment."[2]

Indeed, what makes Walter stand out in the play is his intensity, his big dreams, and his great frustration in not getting what he wants. At the same time, he feels he is not being understood or supported by the very people he should be able to count on—his own family as well as his own race. Ironically though, while Walter is held back by the prejudice of society, he has his own prejudices, which he does not seem to recognize. For example, he tells Ruth she is like other African-American women, who have small minds and do not understand that they need to build up their men. He says African-American people only know how to moan, pray, and have babies.

When Walter is angry and feels overly frustrated, he can be quite cutting. For instance, when George arrives, Walter tries to talk to him about his big ideas since he knows George's father is a successful, rich man. Yet when George will not listen, Walter's temper flares. He immediately makes fun of George for being a college boy, for the way he dresses, for the fact that his school does not teach him how to be a man. Similarly, he argues with Beneatha for not being grateful for the sacrifices the family has made for her education. While he seems correct about this, instead of making his point and letting the argument stop, he adds some callous advice, telling Beneatha she should "go be a nurse like other women—or just get married and be quiet."[3] Aside from prejudiced comments, Walter makes other quite stinging remarks. He scathingly lashes out at his mother, "So you butchered up a dream of mine—you—who always talking 'bout your children's dreams."[4]

These and other remarks show Walter's self-ishness. For instance, when he confronts Beneatha about her lack of gratitude, he is quick to argue that she should not become a doctor. Of all people, Walter, the man who is so intent on his own dreams, makes no attempt to understand his sister's dream or what she would feel like if she gave it up.

Plus, Walter tells Willy he is waiting for the check. He just assumes some of it will be his and does not concern himself about what the others might want to use it for. He takes this a step further and even has papers drawn up for the deal and shows them to Mama when he asks for the money. He hears Mama's reasons for being against his plan but does not think of what she wants or what his own wife wants. Later, when he learns that Mama has put a deposit on a house for all of them, he is not happy for the family, even when he sees Ruth's ecstatic reaction.

While Walter makes no effort to understand the others' desires, he is not completely self-centered. When he speaks of wanting a better life, he is quick to say he wants pearls for his wife, that his son should not have to sleep on a couch, and that Mama should not have to work so hard. He feels he can dream for the others as well as for himself.

Just what is it that Walter wants? One critic
describes it this way:

> Strong, aggressive, ambitious, ruthless even, like the men
> he imitates, Walter reaches for the complete American
> Dream. It is natural that he would, for the freedom that
> America grants an individual holds the possibility of
> unlimited riches, both spiritual and economic. What
> Walter dreams of and aggressively pursues is the power
> that money brings, power being the essence of the only
> kind of manhood he is willing to accept.... However,
> Walter's personal stake in his dream must be balanced
> by the primary purpose for which he seeks it—a radical
> change in his family's living conditions. This change is
> much wider in scope than Lena's planned move from their
> cramped apartment to a larger suburban home. It means
> a wholly different and improved standard of living:
> a substantial move up the socio-economic ladder, the
> complete abandonment of poverty, the chance to live
> the kind of life most Americans dream of living.[5]

But Walter's dream seems more than what many people would be satisfied with. He talks repeatedly about money, and when his mother asks him why he has to focus so much on money, he says "with immense passion" that "it is life."[6] In the same way, when Mama does agree to trust Walter with some of the money and he is ecstatic, he grabs his son and outlines a whole new life for them together. In this life, Walter will be in charge of many offices, and the gardener will greet him after a hard day's work as an executive. Walter will have had to work hard dealing with secretaries who make mistakes and such. His wife will have her own fancy car to use for shopping, and his son will be able to go to whatever college he desires. They will all be very happy.

Walter describes this scenario not only to a young boy but also to the audience. We see many of its flaws, while the boy, still young and trusting, believes in his father's vision.

First, we realize, Walter is making a big leap, assuming he will be able to move from being a liquor store owner to a powerful executive. Also, we see he still has prejudices when he makes his comment about the secretaries and all their mistakes. One wonders, also, about the gardener; will Walter treat him as something more than a servant?

Additionally, we clearly see Walter's belief that money can do anything—it can make his wife kiss him in happiness and it can get his boy into any school at all. Mama's view of the value of hard work certainly is lost here, since no mention is made of how hard Travis will have to study to get good grades. The belief that money can buy anything also fits in with Walter's perspective on spreading some money around to the right people so he and his buddies can get their liquor store sooner. Also, Walter shows a lack of understanding about people, trusting Willy with his money.

Walter is not only a victim of his naïve views

but of his own emotions. Previously, it was mentioned how he readily gets angry, but really all of his emotions are quick to surface and quite intense. For instance, when he believes he will not get any money from Mama, he is so completely crushed that he cannot go to work for days and drinks. When he hears that Willy has taken his money, he is a rush of emotion—disbelieving, angry, inconsolable. But at the same time, being quick to emote has its benefits. When Mama does give Walter some of the money, he is jubilant, a new person, and can hardly wait for the venture to begin, dances with his wife in a fit of joy in the kitchen, and takes her out to the movies and holds her hand. Ultimately, it is this same intense emotion that comes to his aid in the crisis with Lindner. While he believes he should accept Lindner's offer and stay out of the segregated neighborhood, instead he remembers the importance of pride. While he wants so much, he sees that it is pointless to want or even receive if one must give up one's dignity. Walter does not only realize this, he feels it so intensely that he starts to cry as he speaks to Lindner:

> [W]e come from people who had a lot of pride. I mean — we are very proud people. And that's my sister over there and she's going to be a doctor — and we are very proud — … [W]e called you over here to tell you that we are very proud and that this is — this is my son, who makes the sixth generation of our family in this country, and that we have all thought about your offer and we have decided to move into our house because my father — my father — he earned it.[7]

Diana Sands as Beneatha.

CHAPTER 7

Beneatha

Beneatha Younger is Walter's younger sister. She is 20 years old and a college student. She is intense, energetic, feisty, and witty and believes she is right and others are behind the times. She is less wise and mature than Ruth and Mama but truly meets her match in Joseph Asagai, who gets her to see her own shortcomings. While she looks down on her brother and calls him "a nut,"[1] she has some of the same characteristics that he does. For instance, she dreams big, she never backs down from a fight, and she feels she is not understood. In Walter's case, not being understood is greatly disturbing. Beneatha, though, accepts that she will not be understood.

Beneatha stands apart from the others in the play in several ways. First, as a college student, she is more learned, exposed to more, and has learned to love to think.

Her English is notably different from that of the others because of her education. She is interested in the

ASSIMILATIONISTS
People who integrate themselves into a larger group by eliminating or downplaying their own differing characteristics (in the play, those referred to are blacks who try to act like whites so they will be accepted by them).

newspaper, whereas the other women in the house are not, and she has a new-found interest in Africa—its culture and political plight—and recognizes that it is an important part of her heritage. Whereas she seems to speak wisely about Africa to both George Murchison and Mama, she is brought off her pedestal when Joseph Asagai, an intelligent suitor and native of Africa, calls for a visit. He brings her traditional African garb that she has asked for, but when she tries it on she has no idea of how to properly wrap the garments around herself and he must teach her. While she proudly has disparaged assimilationists, Joseph calmly asks her about her hair and why she goes through so much trouble to get rid of its kinkiness rather than leave it natural. Apparently it is something that she has not thought about much. She has not seen her own assimilationist actions for what they are. Also, Joseph's calmness makes him appear more self-assured than Beneatha. In fact, he literally is more self-assured about Beneatha, since he feels strongly for her while she is unsure of her feelings for him.

For the most part, Beneatha stands out because of her education and outside interests that the rest of the family members do not have. At the same time, she is very much the universal young woman who feels she knows everything and is ready

THE AFRICAN CONTINENT

Joseph Asagai is the character who brings Africa to the Younger household. Beneatha becomes highly interested in its history as part of her heritage as well as interested in its current state of affairs and the harm it has endured because of colonialism. As educated as Beneatha is, Joseph, being a native of Africa and one highly dedicated to its freedom, knows much more and teaches Beneatha and hopes she will return to Africa with him. The other members of the Younger family, like many people living during the time the play appeared and even today, had little knowledge of African history or its current situation.

The selection from a speech of W.E.B. DuBois, a famous African-American sociologist and one of the key leaders of the civil rights movement, gives a perspective on some early twentieth-century African history. It is taken from *On Prejudice: A Global Perspective*, edited by Daniela Gioseffi:

[B]efore the Berlin Conference had finished its deliberations they had annexed to Germany an area in Africa over half as large again as the whole German Empire in Europe. Only in its dramatic suddenness was this undisguised robbery of the land of seven million natives different from the methods by which Great Britain and France got four million square miles each, Portugal three quarters of a million; and Italy and Spain smaller but substantial areas.

The methods by which this continent has been stolen have been contemptible and dishonest beyond expression. Lying treaties, rivers of rum, murder, assassination, mutilation, rape and torture have marked the progress of Englishman, German, Frenchman, and Belgian on the Dark Continent. The only way in which the world has been able to endure the horrible tale is by deliberately stopping its ears and changing the subject of conversation while the devilry went on.

to conquer the world. But she still has some growing up to do. Early in the play, for example, Walter criticizes his sister. He apparently believes she sees herself as better than the rest of the family because she has been in school to become a doctor while the others have been knocking themselves out working at menial jobs and making sacrifices. Rather than acknowledging that Walter may be right, Beneatha sarcastically thanks Walter excessively. We see, then, that Beneatha may be selfish. While Walter may not be right to assume that Beneatha thinks she is better than the others, it seems he is right in that the others have made sacrifices for her and she has not been appropriately appreciative.

The audience sees another instance of selfishness and youth in Beneatha, also early in the play, when she says she will be going to guitar lessons. At this point, Walter has gone to work and Mama and Ruth make comments to Beneatha and each other about the lessons. The two older women mostly laugh at Beneatha, who, they reveal, is always taking up new hobbies and not sticking with them. Some of them, like horseback riding, can be expensive, yet, unlike Walter, the women here are not so concerned about the money involved. When they question why Beneatha tries so many hobbies and she replies that she needs to express herself, they really are quite surprised and laugh at the concept, something that seems quite foreign to women who are struggling just to get by.

Another, more disturbing, confrontation occurs between Beneatha and Mama toward the beginning of the play as well. The confrontation points out Beneatha's stubbornness and youthfulness. In this instance, Beneatha says she is sick of God, who does not exist, getting all the credit that man truly deserves. Mama finds Beneatha's comments extremely upsetting and warns Beneatha to stop talking about God's nonexistence or she will get slapped, but the young woman does not stop.

Mama slaps her across the face and makes her state that God still exists. Mama slaps her hard, and there are long pauses that add to the drama of the moment. When Mama then walks into the other room, Ruth tells Beneatha she got hit like a child because she was acting like a child. Rather than realize that Mama has certain beliefs and wants her children to have them, rather than realize that Mama is still in charge of the household, Beneatha has felt it is more important to voice her view. Even after Ruth's comment, Beneatha still must get in the last word and proclaim again that she does not believe in God.

Beneatha does show signs of change, however. In a pivotal scene, she reacts in a way we might not expect. Specifically, the scene occurs when the family finds out that Walter has given his money to a friend to use in the first step in their investing in a liquor store, yet the friend has run off with the money. The lost money is not only the money

Mama gave to her son to do with as he thought best but the money she had told him to put in a bank account for Beneatha's education. All the women in the family had thought the liquor store was a bad idea, and Ruth had also voiced mistrust of the friends Walter had been considering going into business with.

When the family learns the money is gone, Walter and Mama react the most dramatically. Mama is so upset that she starts to mindlessly beat her son in the face. Beneatha, surprisingly, is the one who stops her. When Mama stops, she continues to call out to God for help, and it is Beneatha who pleads with her after each cry to stop. The money for Beneatha's education is lost and she earlier has called her brother crazy and argued with him, yet in this moment, she comes to his aid. It is a noble step, a step in the direction of growing up. Beneatha realizes that the family cannot disintegrate, that Mama does not really want to attack her son, that the situation is bad enough and the family must not make it worse.

Still, the path toward becoming an adult is not an easy one for Beneatha. Although she has made Mama stop the beating, later she says she disowns her brother. At that point, Mama severely chastises her for her lack of sympathy. Here, then, their roles are reversed. Whereas Beneatha had stopped Mama from attacking her son, now Mama tries to stop Beneatha from turning against her brother. Mama returns to being the woman who knows best, and Beneatha appears to not have become as selfless as we might earlier have believed.

Beneatha does go through a reevaluation of her plans and motives, though, as the reality of the lost money sinks in further. First, her perspective on being a doctor changes. As one critic explains, initially "Beneatha had always pinned her personal aspirations and her hopes for a more equitable and compassionate society on the prospect of becoming a doctor, reflecting Hansberry's belief that social idealism—the commitment to a better society—is intimately tied to individual moral obligation: that social justice is the collective expression of idealism deeply felt by individuals."[2]

Yet when the money is lost, Beneatha tells Joseph Asagai that she was overly idealistic and childish to believe that physically fixing people could be enough help, since people are in need of much more fixing. She describes her new, more cynical vision of the world, a world in which, rather than progressing, all people just march around in one endless circle, each person envisioning his or her own "little mirage"[3] of the future. Yet Joseph tells her there is a place for idealists and children in this world, that there is progress, and that all people are traveling on a line into a future of infinite possibility. "And because," he explains, "we cannot see the end—we also cannot see how it changes. And it is very odd but those who see the changes are called 'ideal-ists'—and those who cannot, or refuse to think, they are the 'realists.' It is very strange, and amusing too, I think."[4] Joseph remains steady in his belief for a better world. His speech here and his offer to marry Beneatha make her realize she has to continue to dream and see the possibilities for something better and that dreams should not be pushed aside because of temporary setbacks.

Ruby Dee as Ruth.

CHAPTER 8

Ruth

Ruth is Walter's 30-year-old wife. She is described as having been pretty but, Hansberry writes in the play, "disappointment has already begun to hang in her face."[1] Ruth is the first character in the play to appear on stage. She is a tired but stern taskmaster who prods her husband and son to get up and get ready for work and school. As everyone gets going, she makes breakfasts, checks her son's attire, and starts ironing—all before getting ready to go off to her own job. As one critic remarks,

> *The family member perhaps destined for greatest suffering under the continued economic burden is Walter Lee's*

work-weary wife, Ruth. Her plight underscores that
Hansberry intends the play to confront not just issues
of race and gender but those of social class as well.... .
According to hooks [bell hooks, a famous critic who does
not capitalize her name], black women like Ruth are
objects of oppression: first by black men like Walter Lee,
who must counter their own racial victimization and ...
second by middle- and upper-class white women, them-
selves victims of sexism, who are yet able to exploit their
servants and maids.[2]

While Ruth may be tired, she is still tough
and determined. For example, even though other
characters comment on her not looking good that
morning and even though she has to sit down
before she faints, she still wants to go to work that
day. She also directs her family, determined to steer
them to be their best. For example, she tells both
her husband and son not to be thinking about the
check that is to arrive since that belongs to Mama.

Similarly, when her son stays out too long later in the play, she insists on giving him a beating because he has done this more than once. In her interactions with her husband, she also can be quite tough and even mean. For instance, she does not back down from her view that his friends are no good and his dreams will not get him anywhere. She tells her husband when he criticizes her for not supporting him that other men actually do things, a cutting remark.

But while Ruth can argue intently and disturbingly with her husband, we realize when she talks to Mama about the check that Ruth loves him and wants their relationship to be better. Even though she has told the others that the money is Mama's, even though she has great respect for Mama, and even though she dislikes Walter's friends, Ruth still asks Mama if she can give some of the money to Walter so he can buy his liquor store. Although Ruth knows before the conversation starts that Mama is against the idea, she does not quickly back down when Mama gives her reasons. Like Mama, she feels a gulf between herself and Walter. She is not quite sure how to fix it, but knows she has to try.

Before Mama even comes on stage, Walter says Ruth has a special connection with her. This, in fact, becomes clear nearly as soon as Mama appears. Whereas prior to the appearance Ruth has been giving orders to the family, as soon as Mama arrives, Mama takes charge and Ruth for the most part lets her. It is not just notable that Ruth respects Mama, though. Ruth also is a confidant for Mama. When Walter and Beneatha have left the apartment, Mama asks Ruth about how the two can be so different from their own mother. Mama respects Ruth not only enough to ask her advice but to listen to Ruth without getting angry when she asks about the money for the liquor store. Similarly, Ruth understands Mama's reasons for turning down her request.

Ruth and Mama also have another connection in that they are both mothers, trying to nurture their children in difficult circumstances. The only times Ruth speaks harshly to Mama is when Mama questions how Ruth is treating her son—is she feeding him warm breakfasts, why is she ready to beat him without hearing his side of the story, etc. Ruth sees herself as a good, responsible person and mother and does not want to be questioned about this.

Ruth knows that good family relationships are important. Early in the play, she is giving her son quite a number of orders and insisting that he stop asking about money, but before he leaves for school, she turns warm and playful with him, insisting on a hug, even though she knows he is angry with her. While her son gives in, we see that there is no easy way for Ruth to get on the good side of her husband. It is only much later in the play that we see her and Walter finally break through their anger and frustration and talk about how they used to be happy together, hopeful about their dreams. We realize, then, that at least part of the trouble between them has to do with the frustration they feel from society, a frustration over not having had their dreams fulfilled. Later, the significance of dreams becomes more apparent when Walter transforms into an exuberant, happy man because his mother agrees to entrust him with the money. This, he believes, will allow him to fulfill his dream. Suddenly Ruth finds her husband making her his dance partner in the kitchen and taking her out to the movies, where they even hold hands.

Like Walter, Ruth is concerned about money. Walter dreams about amassing it, whereas Ruth is realistically concerned about what to do since they do not have much of it. Her worry, as contrasted to her husband's view, becomes clear very early in the play, when their son asks Ruth for fifty cents that he needs for school. Ruth tells the boy they just do not have the money, but Walter acts surprised that she could say such a thing to the boy. He not only readily hands their son the money but gives him extra. Ruth is angry, whereas she quickly voiced her anger earlier, here she does not, perhaps realizing that her husband does not want to appear inadequate to his son.

Ruth also is someone who believes in God, is honest, and tries to do what is right and proper. When Walter says it is necessary to pay people off to get the license for the liquor store, Ruth is shocked that he should think of doing so. When Walter lashes out at George Murchison, she is embarrassed and tries to make up for the uncomfortable situation by treating George respectfully and politely.

More significantly, the various aspects of Ruth clash when she becomes pregnant. She goes to see about having an abortion without telling her husband or anyone else, feeling driven to do so because they have so little money and live in such cramped conditions. As Mama later explains, sometimes a mother feels she has to take care of the family she has living above all else. Ruth ends up extremely upset, and when we see her hysterical, we wonder if she really will go through with the abortion. Walter does not try to dissuade Ruth from having the abortion, even though his mother tells him that it is his responsibility to do so. His reaction again shows the great gulf between Mama and her son, but also between Walter and his wife at this point. Not only does he not tell her to keep the baby, but he also offers no comfort or concern.

Ruth thinks and wrestles with various issues such as becoming a mother to another child, how to bring up her son Travis, and how to repair her relationship with her husband. But there is something that all the other adults in the play think about that she does not. She has no dreams for herself. Early in the play, she tells Beneatha that George Murchison is a good catch for the young woman because he is so rich. In short, Ruth dreams for Beneatha. Similarly, early in the play Ruth tells Mama she could take the money and treat herself to a fancy vacation. Again, Ruth is seemingly dreaming for another person. Whereas the other characters think of how they would use the insurance check, Ruth does not think of how she could use it. Early in the play, then, it seems as if the time for her dreaming has past.

Later, however, we see another side of Ruth when it comes to dreams. When Mama tells the family that she has put money down on a house, Ruth nearly explodes in happiness. Her reaction is even more powerful, since we were not given a clue that it was coming. While she has been sensitive to Walter's desire to use the money for a liquor store and knows he is very upset to hear how Mama has spent the money (at this point, the family does not know that Mama has only used *part* of the money for the deposit), Ruth asks him to be happy too. Her reaction stands out further because Mama is restraining herself from expressing her happiness and is feeling her son's pain while his wife does not seem to.

We realize that Ruth cannot contain her joy, that this new home, then, is a dream or a part of a dream she had had but had given up on some time ago. Her intense need for the house becomes even more clear later in the play when the family thinks they will have to give up the house. Ruth cannot bear this and instead insists that they have to keep it, promising, "I'll work ... I'll work twenty hours a day in all the kitchens in Chicago ... I'll strap my baby on my back if I have to and scrub all the floors in America and wash all the sheets in America if I have to—but we got to move ... We got to get out of here."[3] Her insistence over something that she had not voiced a need for before seems to be saying

that we all have dreams and need to keep chasing
after them rather than bottling them up.
Curiously, when she describes what she will do to
pay for the house, she says her baby will be on her
back, apparently showing, then, that the house
or the new life the house will supply will also make
it possible for her to give birth to the baby she is
carrying. We seem to be being told that when a
dream is fulfilled so much more becomes possible.

Lorraine Hansberry in 1959.

CHAPTER 9

Other Works

"All art is ultimately socio-political," Hansberry said. "The writer is deceived who thinks he has some other choice. The question is not whether one will make a social statement in one's work—but only what the statement will say, for if it says anything, it will be social."[1] Certainly, as discussed earlier, while Hansberry's first play, *A Raisin in the Sun*, was a realistic portrayal of an African-American family's life and could be heralded for its realism about this family's struggles, the play also brought to its audience many social issues. All of Hansberry's other work would be rich with social concerns as well.

In 1960, for example, Hansberry was working on a script, *The Drinking Gourd*, that would provide a new perspective on slavery. NBC had commissioned Hansberry to write a television script that would be part of a special series to commemorate the centennial of the Civil War. Hansberry's contribution to the series focused on events at one plantation, where the master is trying to run a profitable business and at the same time treat all his slaves humanely. This proves impossible, however, as the master's wife and son work behind the scenes not following the master's wishes. Eventually, the situation reaches a breaking point. When the master's son learns that a slave has learned to read, he orders that the slave's eyes be gouged out. The master learns of the cruelty and goes to apologize to the slave's mother, Rissa, a powerful black woman, but her heart has hardened toward him. She turns the other way when the master falls, stricken from a heart attack, and dies.

Not only does Rissa not help the master, she takes his gun and helps her son and his girlfriend escape.

The drama, while highly regarded by at least one executive at NBC, never made it to television, however. Robert Nemiroff gave two explanations of why he thought this was unfortunately so. First, he explained how Hansberry not only provided a vision of slavery that would require audiences to pity slaves but to also see whites as victims of the slave system. Whites were not only masters. Masters in turn used poor whites as overseers, victimizing them as well and pitting them against the slaves. To show both groups abused, Nemiroff said:

> That is an act of effrontery far more disquieting because, in the very act of extending a hand to whites, it strips them of their claim to uniqueness, and presupposes on the black playwright's part a degree of liberation, an absolute equality to treat both black and white as if they are exactly alike: that is, in the profoundest sense as human beings, linked victims of a society that victimized both.[2]

The second reason Nemiroff cited the play as disturbing to television executives was Hansberry's revolutionary depiction of Rissa. Rissa does not fit the mold of the stereotyped, strong African-American woman who loved at any expense, was devoted to her master, Christian, brave, honest, and generous.

While indeed, Rissa holds many of these characteristics, she turns on her master, *the* good, *white man who has cared for and treated her* almost *as an equal . . . . In effect, she murders him . . . and in that moment the universe itself—the entire mythos on which stands four hundred years of black-white relations in this country—comes unhinged.*

MYTHOS
A set of interconnected beliefs, attitudes, and values that a group maintains.

It is a simple act. A simple, human, motherly act. . . . And yet here [in the United States] it is cosmic, too frightening in its implications to contemplate, because it says: We are human and if you misjudge that fact you will live to pay the consequences.[3]

Aside from *The Drinking Gourd*, Hansberry worked on three other plays from 1959 to 1964 — *What Use Are Flowers?*, *The Sign in Sidney Brustein's Window*, and *Les Blancs*. Hansberry envisioned *What Use Are Flowers?* as a work for television but later believed it could be reworked for the stage. Although she set it aside in 1962, some called it her most experimental work.[4]

This play departs from her earlier realism and instead is a fable with characters, appropriate to such a work, who are not multi-dimensional but rather more representative of certain types. The play's protagonist is the hermit, who lives through a devastation only to find that the only others that have also lived through it are a group of children that are living in a uncivilized state, unable to communicate and selfishly out for themselves. The hermit, who had

PROTAGONIST
The main character in a play or other literary work.

been a teacher, takes on the task of taming the seeming beasts, teaching them not only the practical skills for living but also an appreciation for the beautiful and an understanding of the range of human emotions. The hermit dies as progress is continuing, but he questions whether the children will remain on the path of improvement.

Some saw the work as overly sentimental, albeit another example of Hansberry's optimism: "The audience of a Lorraine Hansberry play left the theater feeling a little better than when it entered. They left with a little more hope; and while *What Use Are Flowers?* is a momentary failure of craft, it is not a failure of vision."[5]

Hansberry's vision was clear, even though she did not produce a large body of work, as she died at such a young age. Because of her early death, she also saw few of her creations on stage. In fact, aside from *A Raisin in the Sun,* she saw only one of her other plays, *The Sign in Sidney Brustein's Window,* produced on Broadway in 1964. In this play, the protagonist takes quite a different form than those heroes in *A Raisin in the Sun* and *The Drinking Gourd*. Here he is a Jewish man living in Greenwich Village and tired of being involved in one progressive movement after another. He is ready to leave it all behind and move to the Appalachian Mountains where he and his wife can be themselves.

Still, there is something inside Sidney that will not let him forget the world. He takes charge of a newspaper and shortly thereafter finds himself once again involved in politics, supporting a man running for local office. Only after the politician wins does Sidney find out he is corrupt, a puppet of political operatives and local drug dealers. When Sidney hears the politician's excuse for his dishonest behavior, Sidney is again thrown into a tailspin. The politician believes dishonesty is necessary to garner power and money that can bring about good political change.

Aside from the politician, other characters show their moral shortcomings, and even Sidney himself, when trying to repair his marriage, offers to run a favorable review of a friend's play if the play will include a part for his wife Iris. The situations change, however, when one character, Iris's sister, kills herself rather than agree to a degrading request and be looked down upon yet again by herself and others. The suicide proves a wake-up call for Sidney, who realizes, like those in *A Raisin in the Sun*, that he must not give up on fighting, not only in society at large but in the effort to repair his own marriage. As mentioned, the play stayed open on Broadway only a short time (101 performances) and with the great help of Hansberry's friends. Later, in 1972, a musical version was produced on Broadway as well.

While a cause is again taken up in *Les Blancs*, it is a cause foreign to most American audiences at the time the play was written—the cause of ridding the African continent of colonialism. Hansberry worked on the play as long as she could before her death and explained what remained to be done to it to Nemiroff, who finished a first draft in 1966. Other friends and theater people provided input, and the play appeared on Broadway in 1970. Hansberry considered it her most important play. While some critics have also seen it as her best, others saw it perhaps as her most ambitious but not nearly as favorably, resulting in the show closing after only forty-seven performances.

Not unlike Sidney Brustein, in this play the protagonist, Tshembe Matoseh, is a man who wants to leave behind participating in social movements and concern himself with his own personal life. In fact, Tshembe, a young African, left Africa and moved to England, where he married a white woman and had a son. He returns to Africa, though, when his father dies. Tshembe desperately wants to remain uninvolved in the political situation wherein natives are revolting against white rulers and even against whites who have set up hospitals for Africans' benefit. But remaining uninvolved appears impossible.

Tshembe learns his father was a leader of the rebels and these men ask Tshembe to become their new leader. He is pushed to do so, curiously, by a white woman, Mme. Neilsen, the wife of the minister who set up the hospital years earlier and the woman who was a teacher to him. This woman is just one of many characters that populate the play, another of Hansberry's works that contains a conglomeration of complex individuals. The play ends with several deaths. Peter, an African servant, is killed for being a warrior, as is Reverend Neilsen. In retaliation, Tshembe kills his own brother for snitching on the warriors and Mme. Neilsen is killed as well. James Earl Jones played Tshembe on Broadway and closed the play with his grief-stricken cry, not only for the deaths but for the horrid situation in which he has been forced to participate, wherein the victims now have created new victims.

Les Blancs had a short run on Broadway, which some believe was at least partially because of the taxicab strike in New York City at that time. For months after its closing, critics wrote of how they hoped it would be performed. Indeed, in 1971, six of the reviewers of the New York Drama Critics Circle made the play either their first, second, or third choice for the best American play of the year.

Signs outside the Royale Theatre in New York City herald the opening of a revival of Lorraine Hansberry's *A Raisin in the Sun* in April 2004.

CHAPTER 10

The Importance of the Work

What makes *A Raisin in the Sun* special? The answer is actually quite lengthy. First, the play was the first by an African-American woman to appear on Broadway. Keep in mind that Broadway is not just another place where plays are performed. Only the best plays, and what are believed will be the most successful, are produced here. Many plays never make it this far. Additionally, *A Raisin in the Sun* was directed by an African-American man, Lloyd Richards, who would go on to direct the plays of the famed African-American playwright August Wilson and others. All but one of the actors in the production were African American as were some of the investors. The play also won the New York Drama Critics Circle Award, so that Hansberry became the first African American to win the award as well as the youngest American to do so. The play became the first African-American play to gain national attention and was performed on Broadway for so long that it broke the previous record for the longest run of a Broadway play by an African American. (Langston Hughes had held that distinction for his play *Mulatto*, which had opened in 1935.)

Hansberry's play also was praised for its realistic depiction of African-American family life. She showed audiences what it was really like. After World War II, the civil rights movement had gained new momentum. The Supreme Court had stuck down the separate but equal concept of segregation in 1954, yet some still were choosing to ignore it. People had seen on television young African-

American children that had to be escorted into a school by federal troops to uphold the Supreme Court ruling. Similarly, the Montgomery bus boycott had occurred in 1955-56. It started when Rosa Parks sat down on a bus on her way home from work one day. She refused to give up her seat for a white rider. The religious community and young Martin Luther King Jr. realized that with Parks' move their opportunity was ripe. While many African Americans were too poor to own cars and depended on buses to get to work, they were willing to take part in the boycott, and so walked to work or took advantage of the car pools that churches had set up. Eyes were being opened.

Yet aside from showing what prejudice does to a family, both externally and internally, *A Raisin in the Sun* brought up a number of other social issues. For example, the play contained three powerful women, each with a different perspective. These females showed not only Hansberry's ability to create complex characters but that there were new opportunities for the strong, African-American woman off-stage as well. The youngest woman in the play brings the most modern perspective on female life to the stage. Even though the women's movement in the United States was only just brewing, Hansberry showed in her character of Beneatha that a woman did not have to live a traditional life but could be educated and perhaps not even want, or need, to get married.

Similarly, Hansberry had displayed before the American people another pressing issue that needed to be addressed—Africa. Again, at the time the play appeared, Africa was a distant place that few really knew very much about politically or culturally. Hansberry brought to light the issue of colonialism, what was happening to Africans, miles away from the United States, and had been going on for years. She connected the African experience to the African-American experience.

Additionally, even before the movement of African Americans tracing their roots, learning their heritage, leaving their hair in its natural style, Hansberry showed her characters in *A Raisin in the Sun* wearing traditional African garb, connecting themselves to African culture.

By the time Hansberry was working on her screenplay of *A Raisin in the Sun,* its ideas had become even more timely. By then young African Americans had started sit-ins in various parts of the country, risking their lives. Sit-ins were a nonviolent protest against segregation in the South, where African Americans had been relegated to certain sections of lunch counters or allowed no service at all. At sit-ins, African Americans would sit where they traditionally had not been allowed. They were spit at and abused for their actions.

Columbia Pictures told Hansberry that in the screenplay she should stay as close to the

Broadway production as possible yet downplay Beneatha's attack on God and delete all cursing. Hansberry was relieved when her work was accepted, since she actually had feared that more requests would be made for changes and that her intentions for the play would be lost. She knew there was a limit to what she could change and feared that if unreasonable requests were made she would not be able to abide by them and the film would never be released. Luckily, that was not the case. Critics praised the film and enjoyed the fact that the entire cast of the Broadway production was involved in the film as well.

It was not too long after the film's release that the civil rights movement would intensify. The film premiered in 1960, and by 1963 the famous march on Washington took place, during which more than a quarter of a million people gathered in Washington, D.C., to protest unfair treatment of African Americans. In that same fateful year, civil rights activist Medgar Evers was shot dead on his front lawn in Mississippi; four young girls arrived early for Sunday school in Birmingham, Alabama, and died from a bomb detonation; and President John Kennedy was assassinated.

But aside from social changes occurring in the United States at large, changes were taking place in African-American the-ater in the sixties and in the time immediately sur-rounding this period as well. How does Hansberry's work fit into this theatrical his-tory? African-American theater before 1950 had only a few notable playwrights. For the most part, other than during the Harlem Renaissance, before the 1950s most plays about African-American life were written by whites and seen by whites (since

HARLEM RENAISSANCE
A flourishing of black literature, music, and art in the 1920s in the Harlem district of New York City. Also referred to as the Black Renaissance.

The cast of the 2004 Broadway revival of *A Raisin in the Sun* comes out for a curtain call on April 26, 2004.

theater was unaffordable to many blacks). These plays usually reinforced African-American stereotypes. Even some African Americans wrote plays that were similar to those of whites, believing that their plays would not get produced otherwise. In addition to concerns over how to get a play produced, African-American artists had always wrestled with what audience they should be addressing. Hansberry and others decided to address the Broadway audience, an audience she knew was mostly white but whose moral conscience she also wanted to awaken. Later, other writers would take the opposite tack by directly addressing African Americans—confronting them with the need to bring about change as well as bringing heroes of their past to the forefront.

In the 1950s, though, African Americans tried not only to destroy stereotypes but to replace them with new images of African Americans in their true complexity. New subjects were also explored by these playwrights, who showed their disturbance over the poor treatment received by African-American soldiers returning from World War II. They also addressed issues related to the Korean War, McCarthyism, and the civil rights movement. These playwrights urged African Americans to stand up for what was rightfully theirs—everything that the American Dream had to offer. Their characters had great persever-ance and determination, and while protest was advocated, violence was not, although some play-wrights warned that it might become inevitable.

By the 1960s, however, a major shift in African-American plays occurred. Some works became more extreme and rebellious. As Elizabeth Brown-Guillory explained, "Writers of this revolutionary theater accuse whites of perse-cuting or victimizing blacks but chastise blacks for facilitating their own victimization. Plays of this militant theater generally center on violent verbal and/or physical confrontation between blacks and whites."[1] Most of Hansberry's work is not as directly violent as some others' works of the time. In *The Drinking Gourd,* though, African Americans are shown as unstoppable rather than as victims. And in *Les Blancs* violence erupts, not as a tool to be heartily embraced but as one that seems unjust and unfortunately necessary.

Following such works came a new African-American theater wherein writers were concerned with building a new African-American world. Hansberry probably would have been pleased to experience such new works. She herself in *A Raisin in the Sun* brings her audience's attention to what is happening in Africa and shows the connection between modern African Americans and Africans. This transition to a more positive focus would have suited Hansberry, the perpetual optimist. As Julius Lester wrote in 1972 of her and her play *Les Blancs*:

> *It is a masterful play, an almost pure distillation of Lorraine Hansberry's personal/political philosophy. My God, how we need her today! She knew that politics was not ideology, but caring. Politics is that quality of becoming more and more human, of persuading, cajoling, begging, and loving others to get them to go with you on the journey to be human.*[2]

CHRONOLOGY

1930 Lorraine Vivian Hansberry is born in Chicago, on May 19, the fourth and youngest child of Nannie Perry Hansberry, a college-educated woman, and Carl Hansberry, a successful real estate man.

1935 Begins school at Betsy Ross Elementary.

1937 Moves with her family into what had been an all-white neighborhood. Whites in the neighborhood protest and go to court against the family. A state judge rules against the Hansberrys; they appeal to the U.S. Supreme Court.

1940 Supreme Court rules in the Hansberrys' favor. Carl Hansberry runs for Congress as a Republican and loses.

1944 Enters Englewood High School and as a freshman wins a writing award for a short story.

1946 Father dies of a cerebral hemorrhage on March 7 in Mexico, where he had bought a home, intending for the family to move there and live untroubled by racism.

1948 Graduates from Englewood High School and enters University of Wisconsin in Madison.

1949 Studies art in Mexico.

1950 In February, leaves the University of Wisconsin; in the summer, studies at Roosevelt University in Chicago. In the fall, moves to New York to be a writer.

1951 Works on *Freedom*, a left-wing, intellectual monthly recently started by Paul Robeson. Meets Robert Nemiroff at a demonstration at New York University protesting the exclusion of black athletes.

1953 Marries Nemiroff on June 20 in Chicago.

1954 Enrolls in courses in African history, taught by W.E.B. DuBois at the Jefferson School of Social Science, New York.

1956 A song, "Cindy, Oh Cindy," that Nemiroff collaborated on, becomes so successful that Hansberry decides she can stop her other work and write full time.

1957 Hansberry finishes her first play, *A Raisin in the Sun*. Philip Rose raises funds to produce it.

1959 *A Raisin in the Sun* opens on Broadway, wins the New York Drama Critics Circle Award, and continues to run for nearly two years. Variety magazine names Hansberry "most promising playwright" of the season.

1960 Writes two screenplays of *A Raisin in the Sun*; her third version, the least controversial, is accepted.

1961 Movie version of *A Raisin in the Sun* opens in Chicago. Wins a special Cannes Film Festival Award and a Screen Writers Guild nomination.

1963 Diagnosed with cancer.

1964 Divorces in March. Second play, *The Sign in Sidney Brustein's Window* opens. *The Movement: Documentary of a Struggle for Equality*, a collection of photographs for which Hansberry has written the text, is published.

1965 Dies on January 12, the same day that *The Sign in Sidney Brustein's Window* closes.

1967 Nemiroff produces *Lorraine Hansberry in Her Own Words*, a radio documentary. The seven-hour show commemorates the two-year anniversary of Hansberry's death.

1969 *To Be Young, Gifted, and Black*, a play about Hansberry's life and work, opens off-Broadway.

1970 Hansberry's play *Les Blancs*, which Nemiroff adapted, appears on Broadway.

1972 *Les Blancs: The Collected Last Plays of Lorraine Hansberry*, edited by Nemiroff, is published. A musical version of *The Sign in Sidney Brustein's Window* is produced on Broadway.

1973 *Raisin*, a musical adaptation of *A Raisin in the Sun* produced and written by Nemiroff and Charlotte Zaltzberg, opens on Broadway and wins a Tony Award for best musical.

1989 *A Raisin in the Sun* appears on public television.

1991 Nemiroff dies.

1992 *A Raisin in the Sun: The Unfilmed Original Screenplay*, edited by Nemiroff, is published.

CHAPTER NOTES

Chapter 1. Art With Purpose

1. As quoted in Thomas P. Adler, *American Drama, 1940–1960* (New York: Twayne Publishers, 1994), p. 181.

2. "Lorraine Hansberry: A Brief Biography," *Chicago Public Library*, n.d., <http://www.chipublib.org/003cpl/oboc/raisin/biography.html> (April 10, 2006).

3. James Baldwin, "Introduction," in *To Be Young, Gifted and Black*, adapted by Robert Nemiroff (New York: Vintage Books, 1995), p. 14.

Chapter 2. Plot and Other Elements

1. "Housing in Chicago," *Chicago Public Library*, n.d., <http://www.chipublib.org/003cpl/oboc/raisin/housing.html> (April 10, 2006).

2. Lorraine Hansberry, *A Raisin in the Sun* (New York: The New American Library, 1958), p. 115.

3. Ibid., p. 31.

4. Ibid., p. 79.

5. James Baldwin, "Introduction," *To Be Young, Gifted and Black*, adapted by Robert Nemiroff (New York: Vintage Books, 1995), p. 12.

Chapter 3. Themes

1. David D. Cooper, "Hansberry's *A Raisin in the Sun*," *Explicator* 52, no. 1, Fall 1993, p. 59.

2. Robert Nemiroff, ed., *Les Blancs: The Collected Last Plays of Lorraine Hansberry*. (New York: Random House, 1972), p. 10.

3. Lorraine Hansberry, *A Raisin in the Sun* (New York: The New American Library, 1958), p. 8.

4. Ibid., p. 119.

Chapter 4. Dramatic Devices

1. Lorraine Hansberry, *A Raisin in the Sun* (New York: The New American Library, 1958), pp. 11–12.

2. Ibid., p. 12.

3. Robert Nemiroff, ed., *Les Blancs: The Collected Last Plays of Lorraine Hansberry* (New York: Random House, 1972), p. 8.

Chapter 5. Lena

1. Robert Nemiroff, ed., *Les Blancs: The Collected Last Plays of Lorraine Hansberry* (New York: Random House, 1972), p. 210.

2. Lorraine Hansberry, *A Raisin in the Sun* (New York: The New American Library, 1958), p. 125.

3. Ibid., p. 87.

Chapter 6. Walter

1. Lorraine Hansberry, *A Raisin in the Sun* (New York: The New American Library, 1958), p. 71.

2. Ibid., p. 13.

3. Ibid., p. 26.

4. Ibid., p. 80.

5. J. Charles Washington, "A Raisin in the Sun Revisited," *Black American Literature Forum* 22, no. 1, Spring 1988, p. 118.

6. Hansberry, *A Raisin in the Sun*, p. 61.

7. Ibid., p. 127–128.

Chapter 7. Beneatha

1. Lorraine Hansberry, *A Raisin in the Sun* (New York: The New American Library, 1958), p. 26.

2. David D. Cooper, "Hansberry's *A Raisin in the Sun*" *Explicator* 52, no. 1, Fall 1993, p. 59.

3. Hansberry, *A Raisin in the Sun*, p. 113.

4. Ibid., p. 114.

Chapter 8. Ruth

1. Lorraine Hansberry, *A Raisin in the Sun* (New York: The New American Library, 1958), p. 12.

2. Thomas P. Adler, *American Drama, 1940–1960* (New York: Twayne Publishers, 1994), p. 192.

3. Hansberry, *A Raisin in the Sun*, pp. 119–120.

Chapter 9. Other Works

1. Quoted in Elizabeth Brown-Guillory, *Their Place on the Stage: Black Women Playwrights in America* (New York; Westport, CT; London: Greenwood Press, 1988), p. 35.

2. Robert Nemiroff, ed., *Les Blancs: The Collected Last Plays of Lorraine Hansberry* (New York: Random House, 1972), pp. 201–202.

3. Ibid., p. 211.

4. Ibid., p. 213.

5. Ibid., p. 24.

Chapter 10. The Importance of the Work

1. Elizabeth Brown-Guillory, *Their Place on the Stage: Black Women Playwrights in America* (New York; Westport, CT; London: Greenwood Press, 1988), p. 27.

2. Robert Nemiroff, ed., *Les Blancs: The Collected Last Plays of Lorraine Hansberry* (New York: Random House, 1972), p. 31.

American dream—The notion that anyone in the United States, even if he or she starts out with almost nothing, can become prosperous.

assimilationists—People who integrate themselves into a larger group by eliminating or downplaying their own differing characteristics (in the play, those referred to are blacks who try to act like whites so they will be accepted by them).

bulwark—A person or object that protects or offers support.

confidant—Someone that another person highly trusts regarding personal matters.

crescendo—The peak of an increase in intensity or volume.

deferred—Put off to a later time.

despondent—Depressed and most unhappy.

fatalistic—Feeling powerless because of the belief that life is predetermined.

feisty—Being energetic and strong and possibly aggressive.

futility—The quality or state of being totally ineffective.

gourd—A fruit that comes from several plants and is used as decoration or, when hollowed out, is used as a bowl or cup due to its curved shape.

Harlem Renaissance—A flourishing of black literature, music, and art in the 1920s in the Harlem district of New York City. Also referred to as the Black Renaissance.

indictment—A statement of great disapproval.

literary executor—A person appointed to manage the literary property of an author who has died.

matriarch—A female leader of a family or other group.

mythos—A set of interconnected beliefs, attitudes, and values that a group maintains.

protagonist—The main character in a play or other literary work.

symbolism—A literary technique wherein one thing represents something else (for example, a flag is symbolic of, or represents, a country).

transcendence—The quality or state of being beyond the limits of ordinary experience.

World War II—A war from 1939 to 1945 in which the United States, Great Britain, France, and the Soviet Union beat Germany, Italy, and Japan. Notable was the Japanese surprise attack on Pearl Harbor in the United States and the Nazi death camps where millions were killed as part of a plan to wipe out all but the supposedly genetically superior.

1959   *A Raisin in the Sun*

1964   *The Sign in Sidney Brustein's Window*

1964   *The Movement: Documentary of a Struggle for Equality*

1969   *To Be Young, Gifted and Black: Lorraine Hansberry in Her Own Words*

1972   *Les Blancs: The Collected Last Plays of Lorraine Hansberry*

FURTHER READING

Books

Fullen, Marilyn K. *Great Black Writers: Biographies.* Greensboro, N.C.: Open Hand Pub., 2002.

McKissack, Patricia C. and Frederick L. *Young, Black, and Determined: A Biography of Lorraine Hansberry.* New York: Holiday House, 1998.

Tripp, Janet. *The Importance of Lorraine Hansberry.* San Diego: Lucent Books, 1998.

Internet Addresses

Lorraine Hansberry
http://www.kirjasto.sci.fi/corhans.htm

Lorraine Hansberry (1930–1965)
http://voices.cla.umn.edu/vg/Bios/entries/hansberry_larraine.html

Educational Paperback Association
http://www.edupaperback.org/showauth.cfm?authid=93